This edition first published 2016

© 2016 Gill Hasson and Gilly Lovegrove

Registered office

John Wiley and Sons Ltd, The Atrium, Southern Gate, Chichester, West Sussex, PO19 8SQ, United Kingdom

For details of our global editorial offices, for customer services and for information about how to apply for permission to reuse the copyright material in this book please see our website at www.wiley.com.

Library of Congress Cataloging-in-Publication Data is available
A catalogue record for this book is available from the British Library.
ISBN 978-0-857-08678-5 (pbk)

Cover design: Wiley

Cover illustration: Gilly Lovegrove

Set in 9.25/12.75 Frutiger LT Std by Aptara Inc., New Delhi, India

The
MINDFULNESS
Colouring and Activity Book

CALMING COLOURING AND DE-STRESSING
DOODLES TO FOCUS YOUR BUSY MIND

Gill Hasson and Gilly Lovegrove

CAPSTONE
A Wiley Brand

Introduction

Whenever you're feeling overwhelmed, stressed or anxious, telling yourself to 'calm down' or 'relax' doesn't always work.

What can help though, is something specific to do that will provide a shift in focus and perspective. Something mindful; a mindful activity.

Being mindful is about being engaged with the present. Instead of ruminating on past events or worrying about future possibilities, mindful activities keep you focused on what's happening right now.

The activities in this book give your mind something specific to focus on; putting pen to paper, colouring the illustrations, designing patterns and doodles in this book effortlessly engages you in the familiarity of simple timeless creativity.

The Mindfulness Colouring and Activity Book contains a variety of creative activities and word puzzles. Each one provides a balance between challenge and skills. The level of engagement will keep your attention focused so that you are fully absorbed in the moment.

Your mind becomes quieter. You can think more clearly and deliberately. With each activity, you will find yourself slowing down as you focus on one thing at a time. You can become so absorbed in what you are doing that stressful thoughts are unlikely to find their way into your head.

Whenever you're stressed, overwhelmed or struggling to focus and concentrate, wherever you are, the quiet, calming creative activities and word challenges of *The Mindfulness Colouring and Activity Book* are simple, offer a pleasant diversion to help you wind down, feel calmer, centred and grounded.

Zen Doodles

Zen doodles are a form of artistic meditation that anyone can do. Zen doodles turn simple doodles and drawings into beautiful images and unique artistic designs.

Zen doodles start with a border or outline. You then draw a straight line, a curved line or squiggle (called a 'string') inside the border.

Now begin drawing and doodling a series of patterns and shapes around your 'string.'

When you begin creating a zen doodle, there's no need to have an end goal in mind. Rather, allow the pattern to reveal itself as you draw.

Although the creation of a zen doodle is unplanned, each stroke of your pen should be made deliberately, rather than hesitantly. Don't worry about mistakes. Instead of erasing them, incorporate 'mistakes' into the developing pattern.

You can use colour for drawing the lines. You can also colour in the zen doodle when you have finished it.

Create your own zen doodle

Fill in the shapes with your own patterns and designs

Word Wheel

From these letters, make words of three or more letters, always including the middle letter. No plurals, abbreviations or proper names.

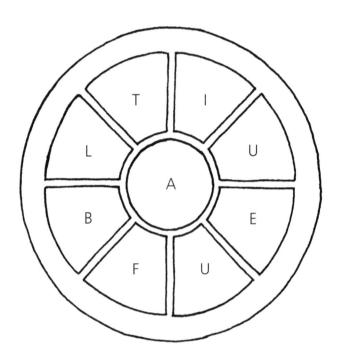

Labyrinth

Unlike a maze, which offers choices of path and direction,
a labyrinth has only a single path to the centre.
Start at the arrow and find your way to the middle.

Continue the vine, adding butterflies and vine leaves

Word Ladder

Change one letter of the word for each rung of the ladder to form a new word. The clues are all there, but not in the right order.

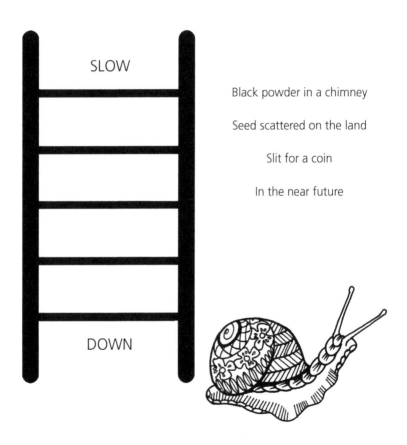

SLOW

Black powder in a chimney

Seed scattered on the land

Slit for a coin

In the near future

DOWN

Word Search: Mindfulness

Find the words listed below, hidden in this word search.
The words may read up, down, forward, backwards or diagonally.

E	N	G	A	G	E	T	A	O	D	G	Y	M	O	F
J	A	S	O	Q	N	D	F	C	X	H	L	M	S	L
M	J	A	X	E	E	O	X	P	C	A	U	O	T	O
I	P	F	S	R	U	N	L	L	C	E	T	N	J	W
N	H	E	G	M	M	E	I	X	Z	T	P	O	K	K
D	R	V	A	M	R	C	C	G	S	J	K	T	A	Q
P	U	Y	S	C	T	T	S	N	E	N	Q	G	U	B
V	J	B	E	N	E	A	T	E	E	B	P	I	M	A
E	N	U	R	E	N	L	I	Z	P	I	E	O	A	A
A	W	W	P	E	R	O	L	Q	A	T	T	T	W	O
W	O	L	S	A	A	W	L	B	X	L	S	A	I	N
A	T	O	L	A	H	T	C	G	A	U	R	Z	P	Z
H	Y	N	O	M	R	A	H	D	U	E	W	W	C	O
L	Y	N	O	M	R	A	H	E	P	Q	N	T	I	U
Y	F	O	C	U	S	N	P	A	S	S	D	O	N	N

ACCEPT	FLOW	PEACE
AWARE	FOCUS	PRESENT
BEGIN	HARMONY	QUIET
BREATHE	MIND	SLOW
CALM	PASS	STILL
ENGAGE	PATIENCE	ZEN

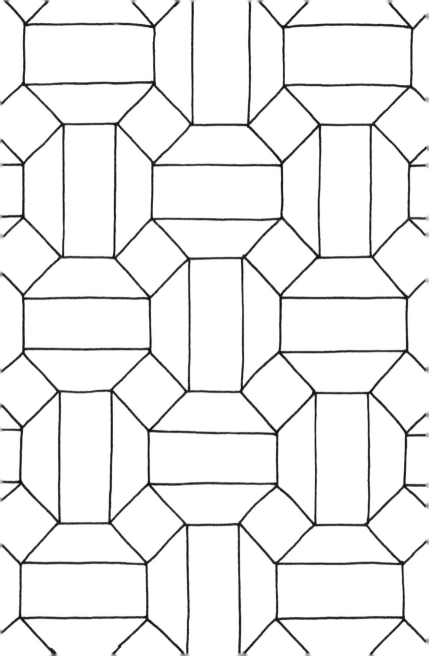

Word Wheel

From these letters, make words of three or more letters, always including the middle letter. No plurals, abbreviations or proper names.

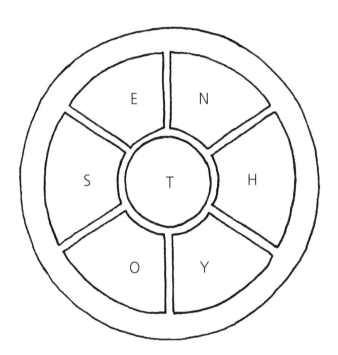

Complete the picture frame and draw a picture – a portrait, landscape, still life or abstract pattern

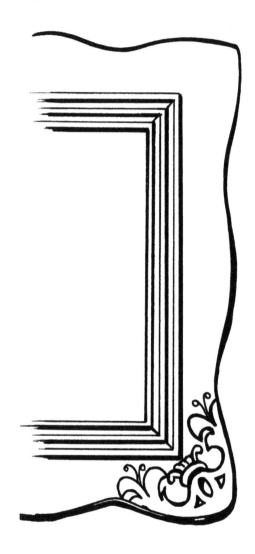

Origami Frog

Cut out the blank page provided overleaf to make the origami frog.

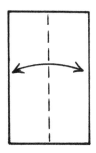

1. Fold the paper in half, and open open out again.

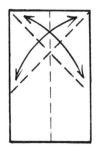

2. Fold both top corners to the oposite edge of the paper then unfold. Your creases should look like this.

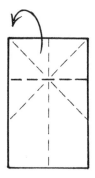

3. Where the diagonal creases meet in the middle, fold the paper backwards, and open out again. It's important that all the creases are clear and sharp.

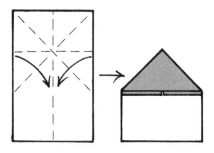

4. Hold the paper at the sides, bring these points down to the centre line, then flatten. The creases should do most of the work here.

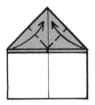

5. Fold the uppermost triangles up to the top point.

6. Fold sides in to the centre line.

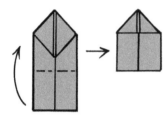

7. Fold bottom of model upwards so the end sits in the centre of the top diamond.

8. Now fold the same part downwards, in half.

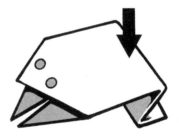

9. Turn over and your jumping frog is finished. To make him jump, press down on his back as shown.

Word Flow

Simply write the word that comes into your mind after the word 'horse'.
Then write the next word that comes into your mind, and so on.

WALK

JUMP

SKIP

TROT

HORSE

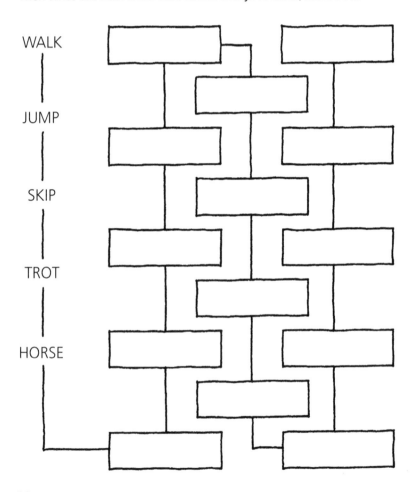

Silhouette

Shade in the shapes with the dots to reveal the image.

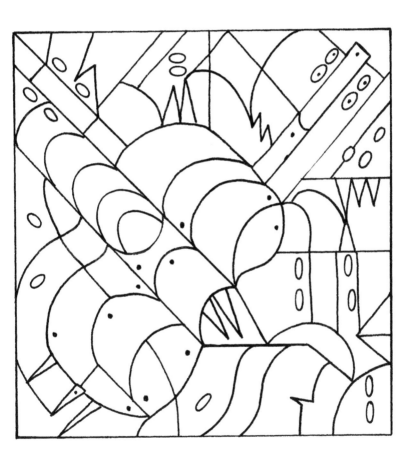

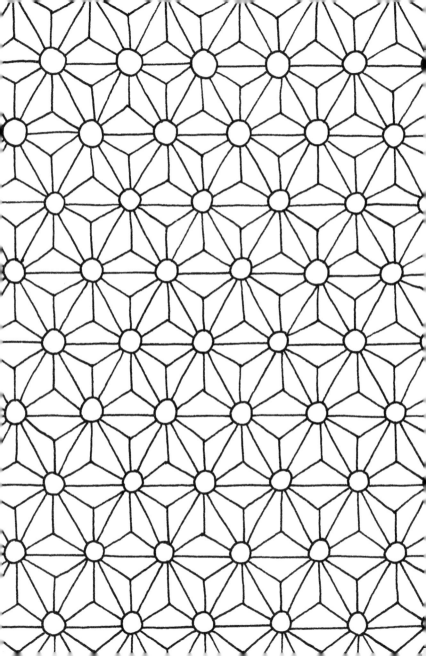

Design your own dream home in this garden setting

Maze

Work your way through the maze, from one arrow to another.

Word Search: Let's Cook!

Find the words listed below, hidden in this word search.
The words may read up, down, forward, backwards or diagonally.

E	R	O	A	S	T	Y	E	D	J	G	B	E	M	Y
Y	T	U	L	K	M	K	E	E	I	R	S	L	O	M
O	N	A	K	P	A	A	S	V	E	I	L	B	V	O
J	C	F	N	B	L	I	E	E	O	L	J	M	N	K
O	R	O	Y	I	A	E	C	T	L	L	R	A	R	S
V	X	Y	O	R	R	R	B	L	S	Z	P	R	Y	X
G	U	I	B	K	J	A	R	W	C	O	V	C	A	M
C	O	D	D	L	E	W	M	F	A	O	X	S	E	A
E	U	C	E	B	R	A	B	C	V	L	Q	I	E	M
O	N	Z	T	J	K	D	H	A	F	T	E	M	D	V
E	A	T	P	M	I	X	B	R	V	O	D	M	B	R
Y	B	K	L	X	C	M	Y	Q	B	A	B	E	W	I
H	Q	L	I	D	S	V	M	Y	O	S	J	R	L	T
B	L	I	O	B	A	Q	K	E	X	T	G	O	K	S
Q	F	A	I	R	T	P	L	G	R	P	M	L	K	Y

BAKE
BARBECUE
BOIL
BRAISE
CODDLE
COOK

FRY
GRILL
MARINATE
POACH
ROAST
SCRAMBLE

SIMMER
STEAM
STIR
TOAST

Word Ladder

Change one letter of the word for each rung of the ladder to form a new word. The clues are all there, but not in the right order.

Citrus fruit

The same

Two wheeled transport

To cook in an oven

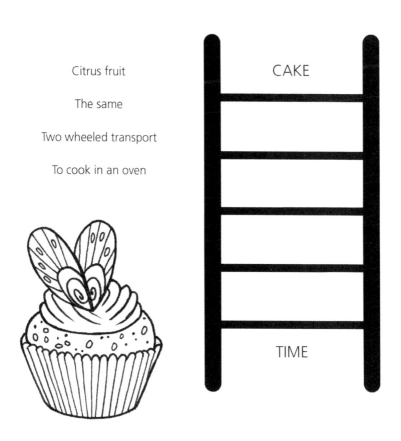

CAKE

TIME

Create your own zen doodles in the squares

Origami Swan

Cut out the blank page provided overleaf to make the origami swan.

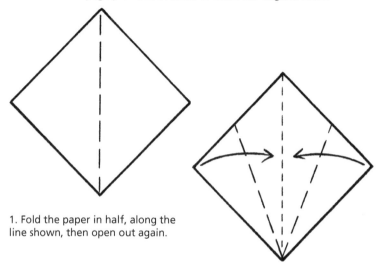

1. Fold the paper in half, along the line shown, then open out again.

2. Fold the outside corners into the centre line, and crease well.

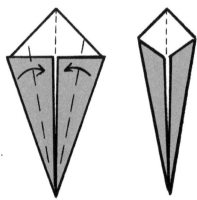

3. Fold the outside edges into the centre once again.

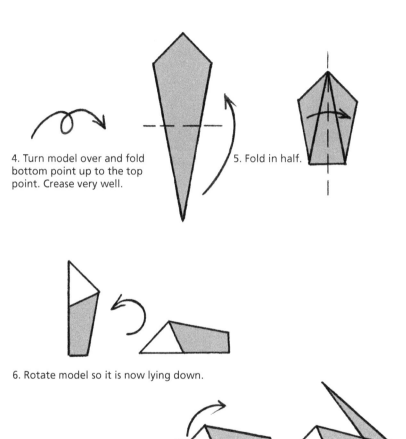

4. Turn model over and fold bottom point up to the top point. Crease very well.

5. Fold in half.

6. Rotate model so it is now lying down.

7. Raise the inside triangle upwards slowly, then flatten and crease well.

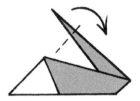

8. Inside, reverse fold the head along the crease shown.

9. Fold each wing upward as shown, then fold it back again slightly. The swan will now rest on its wings and sit up.

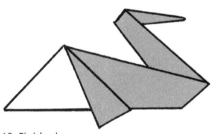

10. Finished swan.

Complete the picture frame and draw a picture – a portrait, landscape, still life or abstract pattern – in the frame

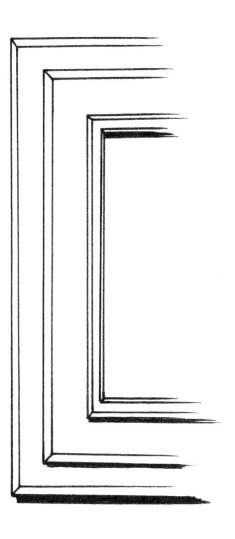

Word Search: At the Beach

Find the words listed below, hidden in this word search.
The words may read up, down, forward, backwards or diagonally.

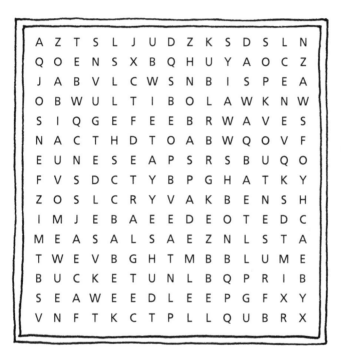

A	Z	T	S	L	J	U	D	Z	K	S	D	S	L	N
Q	O	E	N	S	X	B	Q	H	U	Y	A	O	C	Z
J	A	B	V	L	C	W	S	N	B	I	S	P	E	A
O	B	W	U	L	T	I	B	O	L	A	W	K	N	W
S	I	Q	G	E	F	E	E	B	R	W	A	V	E	S
N	A	C	T	H	D	T	O	A	B	W	Q	O	V	F
E	U	N	E	S	E	A	P	S	R	S	B	U	Q	O
F	V	S	D	C	T	Y	B	P	G	H	A	T	K	Y
Z	O	S	L	C	R	Y	V	A	K	B	E	N	S	H
I	M	J	E	B	A	E	E	D	E	O	T	E	D	C
M	E	A	S	A	L	S	A	E	Z	N	L	S	T	A
T	W	E	V	B	G	H	T	M	B	B	L	U	M	E
B	U	C	K	E	T	U	N	L	B	Q	P	R	I	B
S	E	A	W	E	E	D	L	E	E	P	G	F	X	Y
V	N	F	T	K	C	T	P	L	L	Q	U	B	R	X

BEACH
BUCKET
FISH
ICECREAM
PARASOL
PEBBLES

SAILBOAT
SAND
SANDCASTLE
SEA
SEAGULL
SEAWEED

SHELLS
SPADE
SUN
SUNBED
SURF
WAVES

Silhouette

Shade in the shapes with the dots to reveal the image.

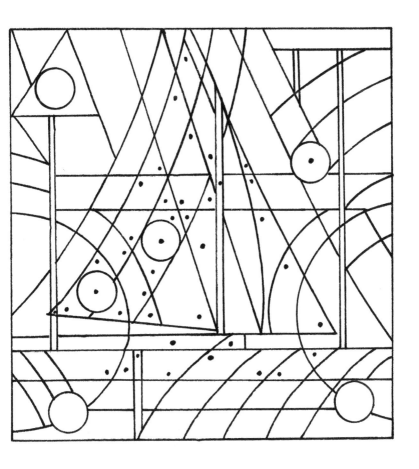

Continue the branch, add tropical flowers and insects

Draw the other half of the vase and decorate with patterns and doodles

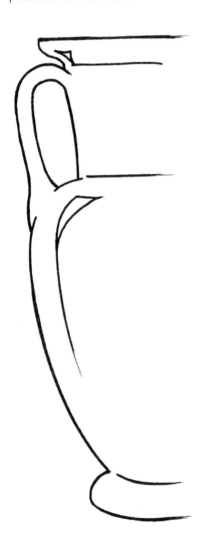

Word Wheel

From these letters, make words of three or more letters, always including the middle letter. No plurals, abbreviations or proper names.

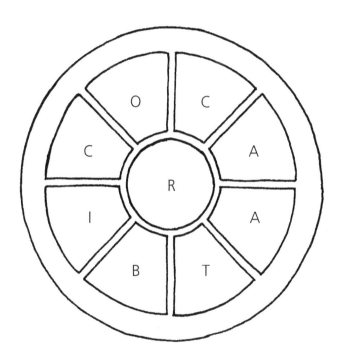

Fill in the shapes with your own patterns and designs

Word Ladder

Change one letter of the word for each rung of the ladder to form a new word. The clues are all there, but not in the right order.

To perform a song

Encircle with a band

Gentle, benevolent

Male monarch

BIRD

SONG

Maze

Work your way through the maze, from one arrow to another.

Word Search: Night and Day

Find the words listed below, hidden in this word search.
The words may read up, down, forward, backwards or diagonally.

M	O	X	L	B	S	N	Y	R	J	T	A	S	Z	T
A	A	T	E	S	N	U	S	K	H	Z	B	O	Q	H
I	F	A	P	D	C	V	L	G	M	J	K	S	F	G
C	O	T	N	F	L	E	I	T	E	Z	U	B	J	I
B	Z	M	E	O	X	L	S	Q	H	N	A	K	I	L
N	P	O	B	R	I	C	R	E	R	G	S	E	N	N
X	M	O	C	W	N	K	M	I	V	U	I	V	P	U
M	V	N	T	A	M	O	S	A	D	E	E	N	S	S
O	L	L	E	S	Q	E	O	C	E	P	N	E	T	O
R	L	I	S	Z	R	S	I	N	K	B	I	I	N	E
N	C	G	D	A	Y	T	I	M	E	L	N	U	N	A
I	B	H	T	H	G	I	L	Y	A	D	W	O	W	G
N	T	T	E	R	L	R	S	K	D	L	A	X	O	I
G	H	B	V	A	U	A	Y	D	N	M	D	C	U	M
B	V	T	H	G	I	L	R	A	T	S	N	U	T	Y

AFTERNOON	EVENING	STARLIGHT
DAWN	MOONBEAM	SUNLIGHT
DAYLIGHT	MOONLIGHT	SUNRISE
DAYTIME	MORNING	SUNSET
DUSK	NIGHT	TWILIGHT

Create your own zen doodle

Word Wheel

From these letters, make words of three or more letters, always including the middle letter. No plurals, abbreviations or proper names.

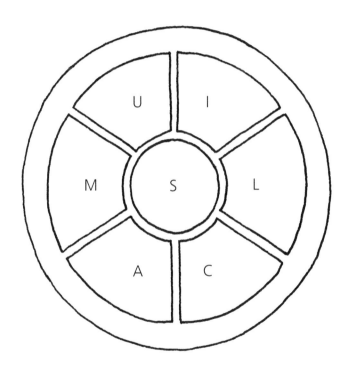

Fill in the shapes with your own patterns and designs

Origami Heart

Cut out the blank page provided overleaf to make the origami heart.

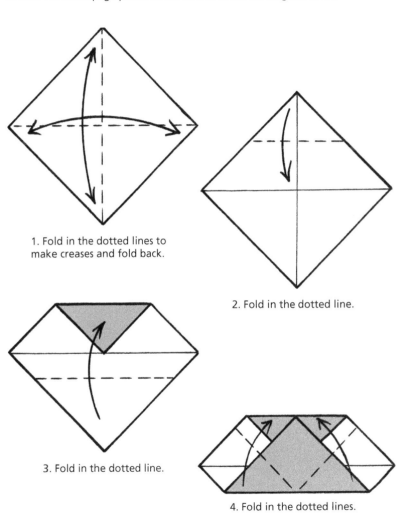

1. Fold in the dotted lines to make creases and fold back.

2. Fold in the dotted line.

3. Fold in the dotted line.

4. Fold in the dotted lines.

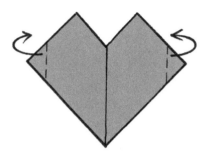

5. Fold backward in the dotted lines.

6. Fold backward in the dotted lines.

7. Finished heart.

8. Decorate the finished heart with your own zen doodles.

Fill in the shapes with your own patterns and designs

Word Flow

Simply write the word that comes into your mind after the word 'roar'. Then write the next word that comes into your mind, and so on.

SMILE

|
|

GRIN

|
|

GIGGLE

|
|

LAUGH

|
|

ROAR

|

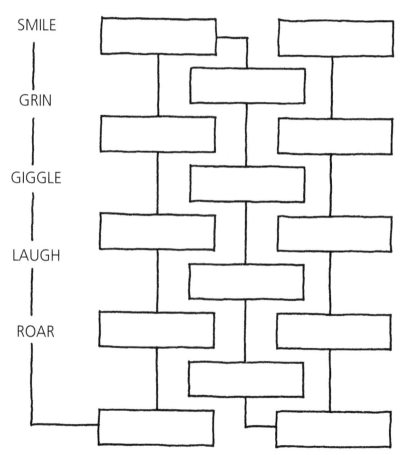

Complete the other half of the vase and decorate with patterns and doodles

Word Ladder

Change one letter of the word for each rung of the ladder to form a new word. The clues are all there, but not in the right order.

Failed to keep

To go from one place to another

Deep affection

Opposite of win

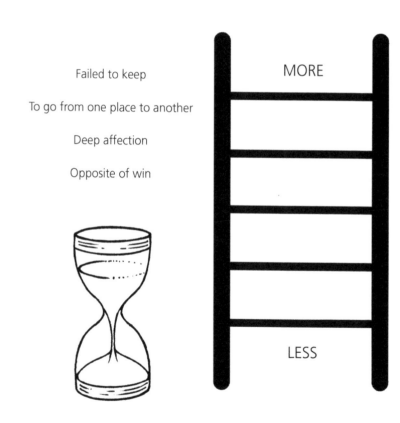

MORE

LESS

Labyrinth

Unlike a maze, which offers choices of path and direction, a labyrinth has only a single path to the centre. Start at the arrow and find your way to the middle.

Continue the branch, add apples, leaves and insects

Answers and Solutions

Word Wheels

Page 10   A U U E I T L B F

Fat Tea Aft Ale Ail Fab Bat Tab Eat Ate Beat Beta Fate Fiat
Bate Bait Flat Fail Tail Bail Bale Tale Beau Able Leaf Teal Flab
Fable Balti Fault Table Fable Bleat Beautiful

Page 19   T Y H N E S O

Yet The Het Hot Ten Toy Sty Ton Not Set Net Snot Host Then
Toe Tone Stone Nest They Sent Shot Onset Those Honest Honesty

Page 57   R C A A O T B I C

Arc Tor Art Rap Bar Car Rot Oar Tar Rat Brit Trio Boar Cart
Carp Aria Brat Coir Crab Crib Riot Rota Abort Actor Aorta
Bract Carob Circa Cobra Orbit Raita Ratio Tiara Carat
Acrobat Acrobatic

Page 69   S I L U C A M
Sum Sail Scam Slam Scum Slim Slum Music Musical

Word Ladders

Page 14   Slow, Slot, Soot, Soon, Sown, Down

Page 39   Cake, Bake, Bike, Like, Lime, Time

Page 62   Bird, Bind, Kind, King, Sing, Song

Page 80   More, Move, Love, Lose, Loss, Less

Mazes

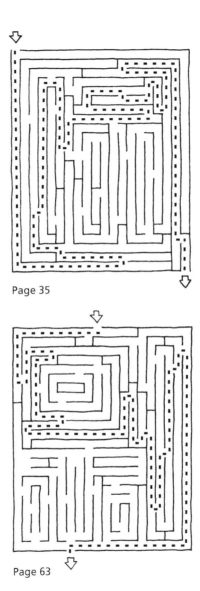

Page 35

Page 63

Word Search

Page 15 Mindfulness
ACCEPT
AWARE
BEGIN
BREATHE
CALM
ENGAGE
FLOW
FOCUS
HARMONY
MIND
PASS
PATIENCE
PEACE
PRESENT
QUIET
SLOW
STILL
ZEN

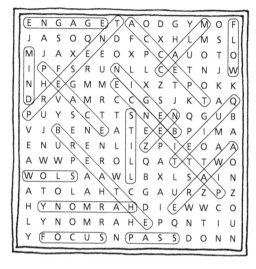

Page 38 Let's Cook
BAKE
BARBECUE
BOIL
BRAISE
CODDLE
COOK
FRY
GRILL
MARINATE
POACH
ROAST
SCRAMBLE
SIMMER
STEAM
STIR
TOAST

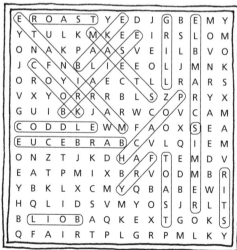

Page 50 At the Beach
BEACH
BUCKET
FISH
ICECREAM
PARASOL
PEBBLES
SAILBOAT
SAND
SANDCASTLE
SEA
SEAGULL
SEAWEED
SHELLS
SPADE
SUN
SUNBED
SURF
WAVES

Page 66 Night and Day
AFTERNOON
DAWN
DAYLIGHT
DAYTIME
DUSK
EVENING
MOONBEAM
MOONLIGHT
MORNING
NIGHT
STARLIGHT
SUNLIGHT
SUNRISE
SUNSET
TWILIGHT

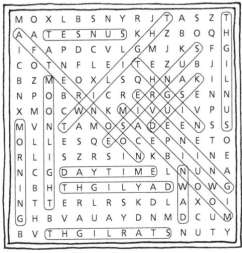

About Gill Hasson

Gill Hasson lives in Brighton, where she teaches, coaches and writes. She is the author of the bestselling books *Mindfulness* and *Emotional Intelligence*.

You can contact Gill via her website www.gillhasson.co.uk or email her at gillhasson@btinternet.com

About Gilly Lovegrove

Gilly Lovegrove is an illustrator and portrait artist. Born in Sussex, Gilly trained at Central Saint Martins in London. She works using both traditional and digital media and enjoys working on a diverse range of projects.

You can contact Gilly via her websites:
www.gillylovegrove.com
www.gillylovegroveillustration.com

Acknowledgements

With many thanks to Keith Lovegrove for his assistance and support with the book. Also, thanks to Andy, Gary and Olivia for their help.

Thank you to the editorial and production team: Vicky, Jenny and Tess, for their encouragement, support and precision.